# Kubernetes

---

*7-Day Guide for Easy*

*Understanding of*

*Kubernetes for*

*Developers and IT*

*Professionals*

Akash V.P.

Akash V.P.

Akash V.P.

or publisher.

<u>Disclaimer Notice:</u>

Please note the information contained within this document is for educational and entertainment purposes only. All effort has been executed to present accurate, up to date, and reliable, complete information. No warranties of any kind are declared or implied. Readers acknowledge that the author is not engaging in the rendering of legal, financial, medical or professional advice. The content within this book has been derived from various sources. Please consult a licensed professional before attempting any techniques outlined in this book.

By reading this document, the reader agrees that under no circumstances is the author responsible for any losses, direct or indirect, which are incurred as a result of the use of information contained within this document, including, but not limited to, — errors, omissions, or inaccuracies.

or publisher.

## About me

The author is an IT Engineer from one of the topmost Engineering Institute (VJTI) where his final year project was based on IOT. He worked in Oracle, for clients like Sumitomo Bank and Silicon Valley Bank. He is a speaker on subjects like Chess and Mathematics. He would be coming up with a few books on Technology based on his experience.

amazon.com/author/akashvp
amazingpublishedbooks@gmail.com

# Table of Contents

An example:

**Kubernetes Master Components**

API Server

Controller Manager

Scheduler

**Kubernetes Jobs**

Creating a Job Manually

CronJob for Creating a Job

## *Chapter 6: Introduction to Some Advanced Kubernetes Topics*

ConfigMaps

Resource Quotas

Persistent Volumes

RBAC

Helm

StatefulSet

Load Balancer and Ingress

## *Bibliography*

Kubernetes Handbook

# Chapter 1: Introduction and Basic Concepts

Kubernetes, also known as k8s, is an open-source system used for the automation of deployment, scaling, and management of containerized applications across a cluster of hosts. It was designed by Google initially in 2014 and is currently maintained by the Cloud Native Computing Foundation. So, what does Kubernetes actually do, and where to use it? Well, it is a vendor-agnostic cluster and a container management tool.

The origin of the word Kubernetes is Greek. K8s means k followed by 8 characters and then s or Kube. It eliminates many of the manual processes involved in the scaling and deployment of containerized applications. You can create a cluster of groups of Linux container hosts and Kubernetes will aid you in managing them easily and more efficiently.

Kubernetes enables the software teams of all sizes, including the small start-ups to Fortunes 100 companies for automating. The applications may include anything from internal facing web applications, such as a CMS (Content Management System), to marquee the web properties, such as Gmail, for big data processing.

For instance, let's say that the application environment is an old school lunchbox. Its content was well-assembled before putting it into the box but there wasn't any isolation placed between any of the contents of the lunchbox. Kubernetes provides a lunchbox which allows you just in time expansion of the contents (this is called scaling) and complete isolation of all unique items in the box. It also comes with immutability, which is the ability to remove the items without affecting other contents of the box.

## *The Need for Containers and Kubernetes*

Before explaining what Kubernetes does, it is important to understand what the containers are, and why people are using them. A container is a small scale virtual machine. It is mini as it does not come with device drivers and other components of regular virtual machines. The most popular container by far is Docker and it is written by Linux. Microsoft has also added containers to their Windows as they have become quite popular. The best way of illustrating their use and significance is by giving an example.

For instance, if you wish to install an Nginx web server onto a Linux server, there are many methods of doing it. Firstly, you may install it directly on the OS of the physical server; however, most people use virtual machines these days, therefore, you may install them as well. Setting up the virtual machines need some administrative efforts and costs also. Another problem is that the machines will be underutilized if you focus them on just a single task, and this is how most people use virtual machines.

It is a better idea to load the machines up with Nginx, a DNS server, and messaging software. People who invented these containers considered these issues and opined that as Nginx or any other applications need a bare minimum OS for running. In that case, why not make a stripped-down edition of an OS, place Nginx inside it and run it. Now, you will have a self-contained and machine agnostic unit which can be installed anywhere. These containers are so popular these days that they are threatening to make VMs obsolete.

### *Microservices with Docker Hub*

Microservices is a popular architecture used for building large-scale applications. Instead of using a single, monolithic codebase, these applications are broken down in a collection of small components called microservices. Docker is an excellent tool used for managing and deploying the microservices.

The reduction in the size of the container is not their only advantage. Containers can be deployed like VM templates. It means an application that is ready to go will require just a bit or no configuration. You can see thousands of preconfigured Docker photos at Docker hub - the public repository. Here, people have taken the time to create some open-source software configurations which may take many people hours or days for putting together. Many people benefit from that as they can install Nginx or some even more complex items just by downloading them from here.

For instance, the one live command that follows will down, install, and restart the Apache Spark, including the Jupyter notebooks also known as iPython.

docker run -d -p 8888:8888 jupyter/all-spark-notebook

As you might have observed, it's running on port 8888, therefore, you may install something else on other ports or even install another instance of Spark and Jupyter.

### *Need for Orchestration*

However, there is an inherent issue with the containers much similar to the case of virtual machines, and that is keeping track of them. When the public cloud organizations are billing you for CPU time or storage, you need to ensure that you don't have any orphan machines there which do not do anything. In addition to that, there is the need to automatically spin up more if the machine needs extra memory, storage, or CPU, as well as shutting them down when the load has lightened.

Orchestration gets rid of these issues and this is

where Kubernetes comes in.

## *Kubernetes Basics*

Google is using Kubernetes since it built the platform some 15 years ago. The very fact that Kubernetes has been used to run the massive systems of Google for that long is the biggest selling point of the platform. Google, a few years back, pushed it into becoming an open-source platform. Kubernetes allows you to deploy clusters, meaning a network of VMs, and it works with various clusters including the Docker.

The fundamental idea here is to abstract the machines further, including the storage and networks, away from the physical implementation; therefore, it is one single interface that can be used to deploy containers for various kinds of clouds, VMs, and physical machines. Here are some basic concepts of Kubernetes, which will help in understanding what it does.

## *Node*

A physical or a virtual machine is also called a node. It is not created by Kubernetes and they are developed by using cloud Oss, such as OpenStack or Amazon EC2, or you need to install them manually; therefore, you must lay down the fundamental infrastructure before you can make use of Kubernetes for deploying your apps. However, from that point on, it is capable of defining virtual networks, storage etc. For instance, you may use Open Stack Neutron or Romana for defining networks and sort of push them out from Kubernetes.

## *Pod*

One or many containers that go together logically is called a pod. These pods run on nodes and they run together as logical units; therefore, they have similar shared content. All of them share an IP address, but can only reach the other with a local host and they are capable of sharing the storage. However, it is not required that they run on the same machine as the containers will span over more than a single machine. A single node is capable of running many pods. The pod is cloud aware. For instance, you may spin up 2 Nginx cases and assign them with an open IP address on GCE (Google Compute Engine). In order to do that, you can start the Kubernetes cluster then configure the connection to the GCE and then type this:

kubectl expose deployment my-nginx –port=80 –type=LoadBalancer

## Deployment

Establishing a bunch of pods is called deployment. The deployment confirms that an adequate number of pods are successfully running at the same time for servicing the app and it shuts down the pods which are not required. The pod can do it by viewing the CPU utilization for example.

## Vendor Agnostic

Kubernetes can work with several cloud and server goods, and this list is growing all the time as many companies around the globe are contributing towards the open source platform. Although Kubernetes was invented by Google, it does not dominate the product's development. For illustration, the OpenStackprocess for creating block storages are called Cinder. The OpenStack orchestration is called Heat. Heat can be used with

Kubernetes for managing storage with the Cinder.

Kubernetes can work with Amazon EC2, Rackspace, IBM Software, GCE, Azure Container Service, and other such clouds and it works using bare metal (using things like CoreOS), Docker, and vSphere. It also works with KVM and libvirt, both of which are Linux machines that are turned into hypervisors viz. a platform for running VMs.

## *Applications of Kubernetes*

So, in case you are wondering where you will make use of Kubernetes, here is your answer. For instance, you can use it on Amazon EC2 even though it has its own tool for orchestration called CloudFormation. This is because you are using Kubernetes and the same command line interfaces and orchestration tool can be used for all the various systems. The Amazon CloudFormation just works with EC2. By using Kubernetes, you may push the containers to Amazon's cloud along with the in-house physical and virtual machines, and other clouds.

So, Kubernetes is anorchestration tool for the containers. They simplify the application deployment a great deal and ensure that the machines are fully utilized. All this lowers the cost of cloud subscription, abstracts the data center further, and simplifies architecture and operations.

Kubernetes is an open-source platform which is used by developers without having concerns about lock-in and it is validated a great deal in the market. Kubernetes provides the necessary software for building and deploying scalable and reliable distributed systems. It supports the container APIs and has these benefits:

1.    **Velocity**: Many things are shipped fast and remaining available at the same time.

2.    **Scaling**: It favors scaling, having a decoupled architecture through the load balancers

and scales with consistency.

**3.    Abstract**: The applications built on and deployed on Kubernetes may be ported across various environments. Developers are separated from the particular machines for the abstraction purpose only. It reduces the number of machines required and so decreases the cost of RAM and CPUs.

**4.    Efficiency**: A developer test environment can be quickly and cheaply created by using Kubernetes clusters and it can be shared as well, thereby reducing the development cost.

**Namespaces, Ingress, and Kubernetes services**: Kubernetes services provide discovery location, load balancing, and naming of microservices. Ingress are objects which provide an easy-to-use front end or the externalized API surface area. NameSpaces provide isolation and total access control for every microservices in order to control the degree to which services interact with the component.

Akash V.P.

24

# Chapter 2: Installation of Kubernetes

Once you have selected the open-source container orchestration platform, the immediate next step forward is selecting how to install the Kubernetes. Refer to the illustration below to have an overview of the role it plays in placement, scaling, replicating, and monitoring the containers on nodes.

1

---

[1]*Install Kubernetes: The Ultimate Guide. (2019) Retrieved from* https://platform9.com/docs/install-kubernetes-the-ultimate-guide/

## *Considerations for Installation*

It is pretty simple to install Kubernetes in small testbeds. You may download Kubernetes from the upstream repositories onto some physical or virtual servers, but running Kubernetes at scale with production workload needs more thought and efforts. Here are the criteria for consideration while assessing the Kubernetes solution for the enterprise workloads:

•**Higher availability**: Does it install clusters that are highly available with the copy of underlying metadata for recovery against failure?

• **Upgrades**: The Kubernetes community provides a major upgrade every three to four months, so decide your Kubernetes strategy, what downtime will the upgrade need and whether it is acceptable for your business.

• **Hybrid support**: Does the solution support the private data center and public cloud endpoints needed for your business to deliver Kubernetes on? Does it offer a similar or same level of SLA and functionality across them?

•**Federation support**: Does the solution support the installation of federated clusters which can grow across public and private clouds for dynamic burstability and robustness of infrastructure?

• **Enterprise readiness features**: What are the additional enterprise readiness features needed by your Operations team to run Kubernetes at scale and support a large number of users? Are they getting the necessary support through your Kubernetes solution? Some of the examples are SSO support, isolated networking, RBAC, and persistent storage.

# Models for Kubernetes Installation

First, let's see the pros and cons of the best available approaches for installing the Kubernetes and some typical use cases. At the end of the chapter, you can also see a comparison between different models.

**1. All-in-one installation of Kubernetes**: There are two all-in-one options described below for installing Kubernetes as a single host for your laptop.

**a. Installing Kubernetes using Minikube**: The use case is Developer sandbox. The pros are convenience, localized sandbox, testing, and exploration. The cons are that it is unsuitable for production, cannot be shared and cannot scale. Generally, any developer's first contact with Kubernetes is on a laptop and with Minikube. Minikube is a single-node Kubernetes cluster which may be installed locally as a VM. The Minikube supports a range of different Oss, such as OSX, Linux, and Windows, and the hypervisors

like Virtualbox and VMware have Hyper-V, and KVM. Here is a diagram that provides certain details on a set-up using Minikube on a single host.

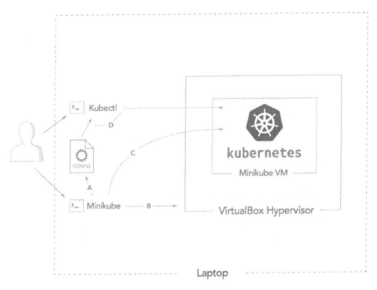

A: Minikube generates kubeconfig file    C: Minikube sets up Kubernetes in Minikube VM
B: Minikube creates Minikube VM           D: Kubectl uses kubeconfig to work with Kubernetes

2

[2]*Install Kubernetes: The Ultimate Guide. (2019) Retrieved*

## b. Installing Kubernetes by using Containers

The use case is Developer sandbox. The pros are its convenience, exploration, localized sandbox, and testing. The cons are that it is unsuitable for production, cannot be shared, and cannot be scaled. Things have been made easy by the Docker to try software frameworks fast in the contained environments as the installation of packages and their dependencies on the container cannot install them on the host. Kubernetes may be deployed as a set of Docker containers over a single host. This host may be a physical server, or a VM or your laptop. The upcoming diagram shows the architecture for Kubernetes running as a container set on the host.

---

*from* *https://platform9.com/docs/install-kubernetes-the-ultimate-guide/*

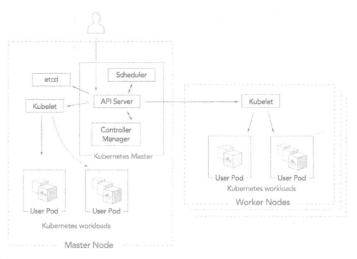

3

As you may see from the diagram above, the Kubernetes components run as multiple containers in the deployment model. Let's see the explanation for them:

---

[3]*Install Kubernetes: The Ultimate Guide. (2019) Retrieved from* https://platform9.com/docs/install-kubernetes-the-ultimate-guide/

• **Etcd**: This Kubernetes component stores configuration data that can be accessed by using Kubernetes Master API Server with a simple HTTP or JSON API.

•**API Server**: The API Server is the management hub of Kubernetes Master Node. It enables communication between different components, thereby maintaining the cluster health.

• **Controller manager**: It ensures that the desired state of the cluster matches with the current state with scaling of workloads up and down.

• **Scheduler**: The component places the workload on the right node and, in this case, all the workload gets placed locally on the host.

### Installer-based Kubernetes

Use is customized Kubernetes installation. The

pros are customizability and scalability. The problem is that it is resource and time intensive, it is YMMV (Your Mileage May Vary) and needs ongoing maintenance. The method normally deploys Kubernetes on 1 or multiple nodes who are

either the servers from the data center or the VMs in the data center or the public cloud. The installers work best for the users that are technically skilled for understanding the underlying design of the Kubernetes. They are capable of addressing and resolving the issues regarding the set-up at any point in time. Users are also required to invest their efforts or use external solutions for enabling enterprise needs like high availability, scalability, and monitoring. The figure below shows one example of the Kubernetes cluster and a master node and several worker nodes.

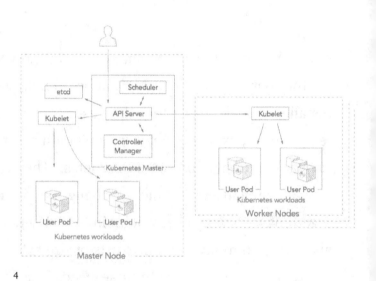

4

## *Kubernetes Having Kubeadm*

The CLI capabilities of kubeadm can setup the

[4]*Install Kubernetes: The Ultimate Guide. (2019) Retrieved from https://platform9.com/docs/install-kubernetes-the-ultimate-guide/*

Kubernetes clusters in a physical or virtual infrastructure. Although the professionals suggest that kubeadm is a simpler way of deploying Kubernetes than kops and kargo, it doesn't

support the highly available Kubernetes clusters. The CLI is available in a beta version since the time of its publication and other components of the installer are in the alpha version.

## *Kubernetes Using Kops*

Another CLI tool is kops which orchestrates the Kubernetes cluster deployment by using the cluster specification documents provided by the users. At the moment, the only supported installation platform for the kops is Amazon Web Services. However, the kops offers other advantages including higher availability for clusters and add-ons, and add-ons for monitoring and networks including Flannel, Dashboard, and

Calico. Users do not need to set up the infrastructure as the kops installs the necessary AWS resources like EC2 instances, VPC networking, and EBS storage.

### Kubernetes Using Kargo

Another CLI-driven tool is kargo, and it is used to roll out Kubernetes clusters and across several platforms like Google Compute Engine, Amazon Web Services, OpenStack, bare metal services, and Microsoft Azure. It makes use of Ansible and needs the users to customize the Ansible state files such as variable and inventory files. You are expected to be familiar with Ansible 2.x.

### CoreOS Tectonic

This is a commercial Kubernetes distribution and is well known for the on-premises installation capabilities. The CoreOS Tectonic comes with support called the Tectonic installer and also the GUI console. At the time, it enables GUI deployment on the bare metal and Amazon Web Services. There are certain products in development, such as Terraform based installation on OpenStack (pre-alpha) and MS Azure (alpha).

## *Build from Scratch*

You may also build the Kubernetes clusters from scratch without using any of the tools. You can also find instructions on the Kubernetes documentation pages about how to achieve this. In case your goal is to gain a thorough understanding of Kubernetes, setting up the platform without help from the above tools will be useful.

## *Using Kubernetes as a Service*

This is applied in cases of multi-cloud and hybrid installations. The advantages are that you get speed, management, scaling and no cloud or infrastructure lock-in. The only disadvantage is that it is a paid service. Kubernetes can also be used by the users as a service when they are

looking for a quicker and easier solution that will allow them to concentrate on building the software instead of managing the containers. Great examples of managed Kubernetes service are StackPoint.io, Kube2Go.io, and Platform 9 Managed Kubernetes.

### *PMK or Platform9 Managed Kubernetes*

The PMK (Platform9 Managed Kubernetes) offers a high-class managed Kubernetes service which works across almost any underlying infrastructure, including the virtual environments, physical server infrastructures, or a public cloud like Azure, GCP or AWS. The PMK is available as a SaaS-managed solution along with monitoring, installation, upgrading, and troubleshooting being taken care of by the Platform9; hence, the operational SLA for the Kubernetes administration is supplied by Platform9.

Apart from the fact that the service is totally managed and works across any cloud or server infrastructure, the PMK has many common enterprise integrations available, such as:

1.      Multiple clusters can be viewed in a single pane.

2.      The highly available and multi-master clusters of Kubernetes which are automatically scaled up and scaled down depending on the workload.

3.      Commonly available enterprise ingredients like SSO or isolated namespaces and the capability to install applications through Helm charts.

4.      The cluster federation which provides a true seamless hybrid environment with several clouds

Akash V.P.

or data centers.

The illustration below outlines the PMK SaaS architecture and its flexibility to work with hardware and cloud.

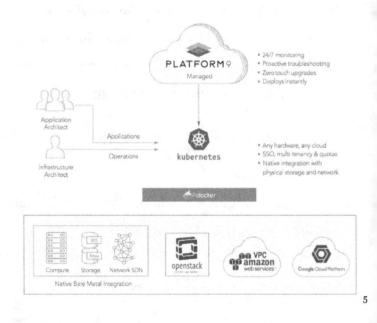

When you are getting started with the Platform9, you can install a free sandbox with Kubernetes

[5]*Install Kubernetes: The Ultimate Guide. (2019) Retrieved from https://platform9.com/docs/install-kubernetes-the-ultimate-guide/*

deployed. Sandbox comes with a guided walkthrough for the SaaS-managed Kubernetes. For creating an on-premises cluster, you need to install an OS supported by Linux on hosts having

Internet access, and then download the installer from a Platform9 host agent and apply it for the host. You may also deploy the Kubernetes cluster on the public cloud, like the AWS, by providing user credentials for the public cloud environment.

You can see a Platform9 Kubernetes UI screenshot below with a cluster on the AWS. You can add new clusters by using the Add Cluster button at the top right of the dashboard. You may also deploy new nodes by using the Nodes tab, and the cloud credentials may be specified by using the Cloud Providers tab.

6

## *StackPoint.io*

The Stackpoint.io comes with integration with a comprehensive set of public cloud providers and you build the container clusters on top of them including GCE, AWS, Google Container Engine,

---

[6]*Install Kubernetes: The Ultimate Guide. (2019) Retrieved from https://platform9.com/docs/install-kubernetes-the-ultimate-guide/*

Azure, Packet, and Digital Ocean. A constant data support is available through persistent volumes and it also includes support for the TPM for

selected providers. The CoreOS is a greatly used OS with the StackPoint; however, they announced additional support for Ubuntu on the AWS in 2017. Users may leverage several Kubernetes native solutions which come pre-installed, such as Prometheus, Deis, and Sysdig among others.

Similar to PMK, the StackPoint includes a cluster federation, a Kubernetes dashboard, and multi-master clusters for enabling highly available applications, but it is not advisable to use server infrastructure running on-premises and in case of data centers with the support of a greater range of OSs.

### *Kube2Go.io*

Although PMK is an enterprise-grade managed

Kubernetes solution by Platform9, they also have Kube2Go.io which is a free community-focused incarnation which allows the users several of the

benefits, such as PMK, for up to five nodes. Although Kube2Go has a free version, it does not have the backing of enterprise support which PMK supplies; however, the users have still available to them the benefits of getting the Kubernetes clusters managed by them and also the version upgrades.

# Installing Kubernetes on the Hosted Cloud Infrastructure

This is used in public cloud installations. Its advantages are scale, speed and management and the disadvantages are security and cloud vendor lock-in. In case it is acceptable to place all your data and workload in a public cloud, the easiest way of deploying and consuming Kubernetes is through hosted services provided by the major public cloud vendors. The 2 main alternatives

available today are GKE (Google Container Engine - although it is abbreviated as GKE for distinguishing it from the Google Compute Engine) and ACS (Azure Container Service).

Obviously, the GKE has been around for a longer period and is more mature. It is a result of having Kubernetes being created at Google. The GKE is only a service that is a part of a huge and sprawling set offered by the Google Cloud Platform. In case you are already using GCE (the LaaSpart of the platform) or GCP, the GKE is only a click away in the Google cloud web console and it integrates with an existing identity and Access Management. While deploying new clusters, you will specify an OS which can be a conventional Linux or an OS optimized for the containers, along with the instance size and the cluster size with a number of worker nodes.

The GKE will automatically create and manage the master node of the cluster. This node is opaque

and is inaccessible. You may access the worker nodes though as they are ordinary GCE instances and you are billed for them.

It is simple to expand the GKE structure by adding worker nodes to the default node pool, or it can be expanded by the addition of extra node pools. GKE gives a stand-out performance in its ability to handle the upgrades gracefully. The API (master node) upgrades take place automatically and transparently only a few weeks after each new Kubernetes release; therefore, the API version of the cluster is kept up-to-date with bug fixes and new features. Although the worker node upgrades have always needed manual use actions, the KGE has recently added a Federation support, thereby allowing multiple clusters to cooperate all across the globe and enabling the highly available and lower latency web applications.

ACS, on the other hand, is a relatively newer offering from Microsoft. Unlike the GKE, ACS

supports several container orchestration engines, including MesosDCOS and Docker Swarm. Surprisingly, the Kubernetes support did not arrive until February 2017. As compared to the GKE, the ACS Kubernetes quality will probably take longer to raise to the same level, or match the depth in features and maturity. There is a downside which is the need to support the other container engines and it limits the ACS team capability to optimize and build the Kubernetes product; however, the ACS might prove to be an interesting option for the users interested in running the .NET applications on the Windows Server OS. Kubernetes and Docker both support Windows, but it is new and yet evolving. If there is one company which will champion and pour resources into it, it is Microsoft; therefore, it will not be a surprise if ACS is to evolve into an excellent, if not exclusive, choice for running the Windows workload on Kubernetes. The illustration below summarizes the installment

model for the two public clouds.

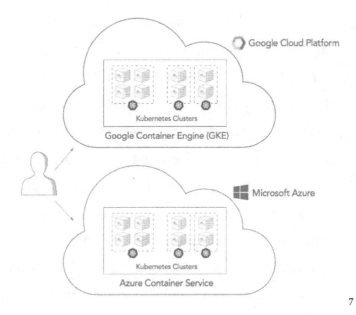

[7]*Install Kubernetes: The Ultimate Guide. (2019) Retrieved from* *https://platform9.com/docs/install-kubernetes-the-ultimate-guide/*

## *A Comparison Between all the Kubernetes Deployment Models*

In this chapter, we have seen all the major Kubernetes installation models; however, the ideal installation model is dependent on your specific requirement and goals. Here is a short comparison of the alternatives available, and their pros and cons in short:

| | Developer Installs | | Kubernetes Installer | | | | Kubernetes as a service | | | Kubernetes hosted infrastructure | |
|---|---|---|---|---|---|---|---|---|---|---|---|
| | Minikube | Docker | kubeadm | kops | kargo | CoreOS Tectonic | PMK | StackPoint.io | Kube2 Go.io | GKE | ACS |
| **Supported Infrastructure** | | | | | | | | | | | |
| Laptops | ✓ | ✓ | ✓ | | | | | | | | |
| Data-Center/ Colocated Hardware | | | ✓ | | ✓ | ✓ | ✓ | | | | |
| Public clouds | | | ✓ | ✓* | ✓ | ✓ | ✓ | ✓ | ✓ | ✓ | ✓ |
| Hybrid Deployments# | | | | | | | ✓* | | | | |
| **Lifecycle Management** | | | | | | | | | | | |
| Built-In Monitoring | | | | | | | ✓ | ✓ | ✓ | ✓ | ✓ |
| Commercial Support/SLA | | | | | | ✓ | ✓ | ✓ | | ✓ | ✓ |
| Kubernetes Upgrades | | | | ✓ | ✓ | ✓ | ✓ | ✓ | ✓ | ✓ | ✓ |
| **Enterprise-Readiness** | | | | | | | | | | | |
| Cluster High Availability | | | | ✓ | ✓ | ✓ | ✓ | ✓ | ✓ | ✓ | ✓ |
| RHEL, CentOS & Ubuntu Node OS Support | ✓ | ✓ | ✓ | | ✓ | ✓ | ✓ | ✓* | ✓ | | |
| SSO integration | | | | | | ✓ | ✓ | | | ✓ | |
| Isolated Networking/ Network Policies | ✓ | ✓ | ✓ | ✓ | ✓ | ✓ | ✓ | ✓ | | | |
| Dynamic Persistent Volumes | | | ✓ | ✓ | ✓ | | ✓ | ✓ | ✓ | ✓ | ✓ |
| Federation | | | | | | | ✓* | ✓ | ✓* | ✓ | |

8

[8] *Install Kubernetes: The Ultimate Guide. (2019) Retrieved from* https://platform9.com/docs/install-kubernetes-the-ultimate-guide/

# Chapter 3: The Kubernetes Architecture

The containers have quickly become a significant way of developing applications as they give you packages that include everything needed for running your application. Now, let's discuss Kubernetes architecture and its moving parts. We will see the key elements of Kubernetes and what their roles and responsibilities are in the Kubernetes architecture. Kubernetes is written on Golang, which is a massive community as it was first developed by Google and was donated to CNCF later. Kubernetes is capable of grouping any number of containers in a logical unit for deploying and managing them.

## *Kubernetes Components and Architecture*

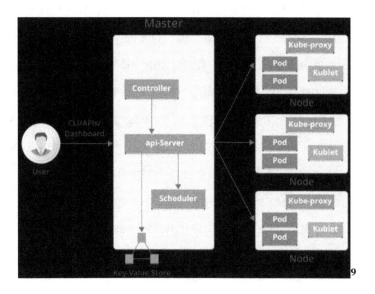

The main components of Kubernetes architecture are master nodes, worker/slave nodes, and the distributed key-value store, also called etcd.

**1. Master Node**: This is the access point for all

---

[9]*Samarpit.*Understanding Kubernetes Architecture.(2018) Retrieved from
https://www.edureka.co/blog/kubernetes-architecture/

the administrative tasks and is accountable for handling the Kubernetes cluster. It is possible to have more than a single master node in a cluster for checking the fault tolerance. Having more than a single node places the system in a high availability mode. In it, one of them will be your main node that will perform all the required tasks. For the cluster state management, Kubernetes uses the etcd which has all the master nodes connected to it. We have already discussed the 4 components of the master node in Chapter 2. Let's see some relevant information again:

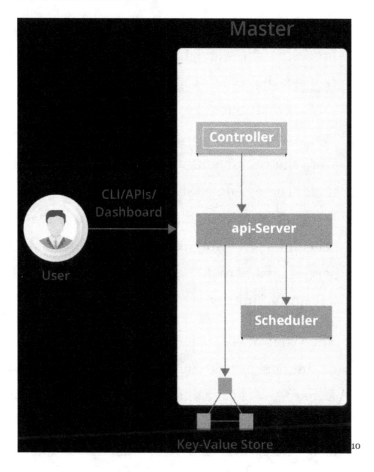

The API server performs all the admin tasks by using the API server in the master node. In it,

[10]*Samarpit.*Understanding Kubernetes Architecture.(2018) Retrieved from https://www.edureka.co/blog/kubernetes-architecture/

REST commands are sent to the API server that processes and validates your requests. After the request, the resulting state of your cluster is stored in your distributed key-value store. The scheduler will schedule the tasks of the slave nodes. It will store the resource use information for every slave node. The scheduler also schedules the work in the form of services and pods. Before the task scheduling, it will also take into account the service quality requirements, affinity, data locality, and anti-affinity etc.

The controller managers are also known as controllers. It is an entity that controls the Kubernetes cluster and manipulates various non-terminating control loops. The controller manager also performs lifecycle functions like the namespace creation, cascading deletion garbage collection, terminated pod garbage collection, event garbage collection, and node garbage collection. The controller basically keeps an eye on the required state of objects it is managing and also watches the current state via the API server. In case the current state of objects it manages is not up to scratch, then the control loop takes corrective measures to ensure that the current state is the same as that required.

A distributed key-value store that stores the state of a cluster is called etcd. Etcd may be a part of Kubernetes master or it may be configured externally. It is written in Golang or Go programming language. Apart from storing the cluster state in Kubernetes, it is also used for storing configuration details like ConfigMaps, Subnets, and Secrets. The raft is a consensus algorithm which is designed as a Paxos alternative. A consensus issue involves several servers agreeing on values and, as a result, a common issue arises in the form of replicated state machines. The raft will decide 3 different roles viz. Candidate, Follower, and Leader. The consensus is achieved through the leader.

Now that we have seen the meaning of the master node and its functioning, let's check the meaning and components of the worker node.

**2. Worker Node**: This is a physical server, or you might say a VM, that runs various applications by using Pods or a Pod scheduling units controlled by the master node. On the worker node the physical server pods get scheduled. In order to access the applications from the external world, we are connected to the nodes. Let's see some of its components:

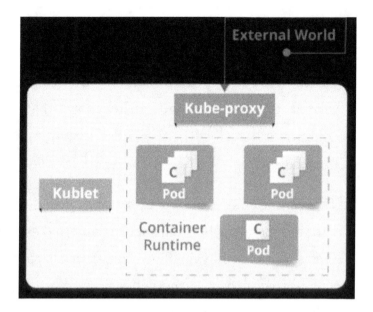

11

Container runtime on your worker node is needed for running and managing the lifecycle of a container. Docker is also referred to as container runtime many times; however, more precisely the Docker is a platform used by the containers for the container runtime. Kubelet is an agent that

11*Samarpit.*Understanding Kubernetes Architecture.(2018) Retrieved from https://www.edureka.co/blog/kubernetes-architecture/

communicates with the master node and executes on the worker nodes. It renders pod specifications via the API server and executes the containers related to the pod and makes sure that the containers described in the pod are running and are healthy.

The Kube-proxy runs on every node for dealing with independent host sub-netting and makes sure that services are available to the external parties. Kube-proxy serves as the network proxy and load balancer for services on the single worker node and achieves network routing for the UDP and TCP packets. This network proxy runs on every worker node and listens to your API server for every service endpoint creation or deletion. For every service endpoint, the Kube-proxy sets up some routes for them to avail.

The pod is one or a set of containers which logically gets together. The pods run on nodes and they run together as a logical unit; therefore, they have the same shared content and they all share the exact same IP address, but they can reach other pods only through a localhost and through the shared storage. It is not desired to have all the pods running on the same machine because the containers are spanned out on more than a single machine. A single node can run several nodes.

## *Using Kubernetes in Production for Luminis Technologies! A Use Case!*

Luminis is a software technology organization that uses AWS for installing their applications. For installing the applications, the company needed custom scripts and tools for automating and it was not easy for the teams other than the operations. They had small teams which did not have the resources to learn the details about tools and scripts. The main problem was that there was no unit of deployment, and that created a gap between the operations and the development teams. The solution was to employ Kubernetes. Let's see how they used Kubernetes:

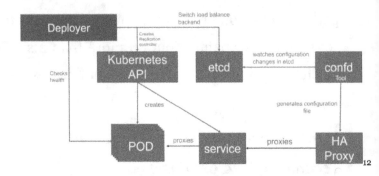

They used the blue-green deployment mechanism for reducing the difficulty and complexity involved in handling several concurrent versions. This is because there is always just a single version of the application running in the background. In it, a component known as Deployer which orchestrated the deployment was created by the team by open-sourcing the implementation under Apache License as a part of the Amdatu umbrella project.

---

[12] *Samarpit.* Understanding Kubernetes Architecture.(2018) Retrieved from https://www.edureka.co/blog/kubernetes-architecture/

The mechanism performed health check-ups on the pods before reconfiguring the load balancer. This was because they wished every component that was installed to provide health check-ups.

## *Automating the Deployments*

Having the Deployer in place resulted in them being able to engage in deployments for building the pipeline. After every successful build, the build server pushed a new Docker image to the registry on the Docker Hub. After this, the build server invoked their Deployer for automatically deploying the newer version to the test environment. This same image was promoted to production by instigating the Deployer in the production environment.

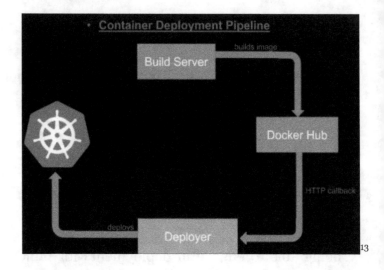

That is Kubernetes architecture in simple words.

[13]*Samarpit.*Understanding Kubernetes Architecture.(2018) Retrieved from https://www.edureka.co/blog/kubernetes-architecture/

# Chapter 4: Understanding the Kubernetes Objects

The Kubernetes objects are constant entities in a Kubernetes system. It uses the entities for representing the cluster state. More specifically they will describe:

- Which containerized applications are running, and on what nodes?

- The resources available for the applications.

- The policy around which the applications behave like restart policies, fault tolerance, and upgrades.

The Kubernetes object is a record of intention. Once the object has been created, the Kubernetes system will work continuously to make sure that the object will exist. By creating the object, you are in fact telling the Kubernetes system that this is the way you wish the cluster should look like, or it is the desired state of the cluster. For working with the Kubernetes objects, whether for creating, modifying, or deleting them, you will have to use Kubernetes API. If you use the kubect1 command line interface, for instance, CLI makes the compulsory Kubernetes API calls needed. You may also use Kubernetes API directly in the programs by using one of the client libraries.

## *Object Spec and Object Status*

All Kubernetes objects include 2 nested object fields which govern the object configuration. These objects are object status and object spec. It is necessary to provide the object spec. It describes the desired state of the object and this is the property you wish for the object to have. Status, on the other hand, describes the actual state of your object and it is supplied and updated by your Kubernetes system. At any point in time, the Kubernetes Control Plane readily manages the actual state of the object in order to match the required state that you supplied.

For instance, Kubernetes Deployment is one object which represents the application running on the cluster. If you create the Deployment you must set the Deployment spec for specifying that you wish for 3 replicas of the application to be running. The Kubernetes system goes through the Deployment spec and begins 3 instances of the desired application in the process updating the status for matching your spec. In case any of the instances are to fail or there is a status change, the Kubernetes system will respond to the difference between status and spec by making corrections and, in this case, by starting a replacement instance.

### Describing the Kubernetes Objects

If you create an object in Kubernetes, you need to

provide the object spec which describes the desired state, as well as the basic info about that object like the name. Once you make use of Kubernetes API for creating an object which could be via kubect1 or directly, the API request needs to include the info like JSON in your request body. More often than not, the information is to be provided to kubect1 in a .yam1 file. The kubect1 turns the information to JSON while making the API request. Let's see an example. Here the .yam1 file shows the required fields and the object spec for the Kubernetes Deployment:

```
apiVersion:apps/v1# for versions before
1.9.0 use apps/v1beta2
kind:Deployment
metadata:
name:nginx-deployment
spec:
selector:
matchLabels:
app:nginx
```

```
replicas:2# tells deployment to run 2 pods
matching the template
template:
metadata:
labels:
app:nginx
spec:
containers:
-name:nginx
image:nginx:1.7.9
ports:
-containerPort:80
```

One way of creating the Deployment by using a .yaml file, such as the one above, is by using the kubectl create command on the kubectl command line interface by passing the .yaml file as an argument. For instance:

$ kubectl create -f https://k8s.io/examples/application/deployment.yaml --record

Its output is similar to this:

deployment.apps/nginx-deployment created[14]

## Necessary Fields

In your .yam! file of the Kubernetes object you wish to create, you will have to set values for these following fields:

- apiVersion - What version of Kubernetes API are you using for creating the object?

- kind - What kind of objects do you wish to create?

- metadata - The data which helps in identifying an object uniquely and includes a name string, an optional namespace, and

---

[14]*Understanding Kubernetes Objects (2019).Retrieved from*
*https://kubernetes.io/docs/concepts/overview/working-with-objects/kubernetes-objects/*

UID.

You will also be required to provide the object spec field. The exact format of this object spec varies with different Kubernetes objects and contains nested fields which are specific to the object. Kubernetes API references are available online which can help you find the spec format for the objects you may create using Kubernetes.

## *Pods*

Pods are the basic building blocks of Kubernetes. It is the simplest and smallest unit in the Kubernetes object model which you may deploy or create. The pods represent running processes on the cluster. It contains an application container or, in many cases, several containers, a unique network IP, storage resources, and an option that will govern how the containers will run. It is a unit of deployment. A single example of an application in Kubernetes that might contain a single container or number of them which are tightly coupled and share resources. As we have seen,Docker is the most commonly used container in Kubernetes Pod, but the pods also support other container runtimes. There are two major ways of using pods in a Kubernetes cluster.

There are pods that run on single containers. This model has a single container per pod and is the most commonly used Kubernetes example. In this case, the pod is like a wrapper around the container and Kubernetes will manage pods instead of the containers directly. The pods running on several containers must work together. The pod may encapsulate an application made of several containers which are tightly coupled and are required to share resources. These containers, which are co-located, may form a single cohesive unit of service. The one container will serve files from a shared volume to the public, whereas a separate sidecar container will refresh or update these files. The pod will wrap these containers and storage resources together in a single entity.

All the pods are meant to run as a single instance for any application. In case you wish to scale the application horizontally that is, or wish to run several instances, you must use multiple pods, one for every instance. This is referred to as replication in Kubernetes. The replicated pods are normally developed and managed as a group by the abstraction called the controller.

### *Volumes*

The on-disk files of a container are ephemeral and this presents some issues for the non-trivial applications while running in containers. First is, if a container crashes, the Kubelet restarts it, and the files are lost. The container starts having a clean slate. The second is that while running containers together in a pod, it is mandatory to share various files between the containers. The volume abstraction of Kubernetes solves both these issues.

The Docker also uses a volume although the concept is loose and not well managed. Volume, in the case of Docker, is just a directory on the disk or in a container. Docker, nowadays, provides volume drivers; however, its functionality is limited at the moment. Just a single volume driver is permitted for every container and you cannot pass parameters to it.

On the other hand, the Kubernetes volume comes with an explicit lifetime. It is the same as the pod which encloses it. Consequently, the volume outlives the containers which run within the pod and the data gets preserved across the container restarts. When a pod ceases to exist, the volume will be diminished as well; however, more significantly, the Kubernetes supports different kinds of volumes and the pod can utilize a number of them at the same time.

Volume is just a directory at its core with some data in it possibly and it is accessible to the containers in a pod. The specific volume type used determines how the directory comes to be, what its contents are, and the medium which backs it. For using the volume, the pod specifies which volume to provide to the pod (e.g. spec. volumes field) and where to mount them in the containers (e.g. spec.containers.volumeMounts field).

The process of a container will see a file system view that is composed of their Docker image and the volumes. The Docker image is the root of your file system hierarchy and the volumes are mounted on the specific paths within this image. These volumes do not mount on other volumes or have links for other volumes. Every container in a pod must specify independently where to mount every volume.

## *Namespaces*

Kubernetes supports the combination of several virtual clusters backed by the same physical server. The virtual clusters are termed as namespaces. They are intended to be used in an environment which has several users spread across many teams or projects. For the clusters having just a few to dozens of users, you do not need to create or even think about creating namespaces. You can begin using the namespaces when you require the features they provide.

The namespaces provide the scope for names. The names of different resources have to be unique in a namespace but not across many namespaces. They are basically a method to divide the cluster resources into several users. The newer versions of Kubernetes will have the objects of the same namespace the same access control policies by default. It's necessary to utilize several namespaces for separating the slightly varying resources like different versions of the same software. You can use labels for distinguishing resources in a namespace.

# Chapter 5: Some Higher Level Kubernetes Concepts

## ReplicaSets

The main purpose of the ReplicaSet is to maintain stable sets of replica pods running at some point in time. It is used many times to ensure the availability of specific numbers of identical pods. It is defined with fields, such as a selector, which specifies the way of identifying the pods it can acquire. It also specifies the number of replicas showing the number of pods it must be maintaining, and a pod template which specifies the data about the new pods needed to meet the criteria of the number of replicas. The ReplicaSet achieves its goal by creating and deleting the pods as required for reaching the necessary number. When the ReplicaSet wishes to create a new pod, it will use the pod template.

The ReplicaSet uses its selector for identifying new pods for acquisition. In case there is a pod which has no OwnerReference, or in case the OwnerReference is not a controller, and, along with the selector of ReplicaSet, it will get acquired by the specified ReplicaSet. Although the replica set ensures that a specific number of pod replicas are running at a specific time, deployment is a high-level concept which is used to manage ReplicaSets. It provides declarative updates to the pods with a range of other features, so it is recommended that Deployments are used rather than using ReplicaSets directly unless, of course, you need custom update orchestration or do not need any updates at all. It means that you might not need to manage the ReplicaSet objects ever. Rather, make use of Deployment and define the application in the spec section.

***An example:***

```
apiVersion: apps/v1

kind: ReplicaSet

metadata:

name: frontend

labels:

app: guestbook

tier: frontend

spec:

  # modify replicas according to your case

replicas: 3

selector:

matchLabels:

tier: frontend
```

```
template:

metadata:

labels:

tier: frontend

spec:

containers:

    - name: php-redis

image: gcr.io/google_samples/gb-frontend:v3
```

Saving the manifest in frontend.yaml and submitting to Kubernetes cluster creates the defined ReplicaSet and pods it will manage.

```
kubectl                create                -f
http://k8s.io/examples/controllers/frontend.yaml
```

With this, you can have the current ReplicaSets deployed.

kubectl get rs

See the front end you created with this:

| NAME | DESIRED | CURRENT | READY | AGE |
|------|---------|---------|-------|-----|
| frontend | 3 | 3 | 3 | 6s |

You may also check on the ReplicaSet state with this:

kubectl describe rs/frontend

This will allow you to see the output such as:,

Name:        frontend

Namespace:   default

Selector:       tier=frontend,tier in (frontend)

Labels:                 app=guestbook

                tier=frontend

Annotations: <none>

Replicas:       3 current / 3 desired

Pods Status:  3 Running / 0 Waiting / 0 Succeeded / 0 Failed

Pod Template:

  Labels:     app=guestbook

tier=frontend

  Containers:

php-redis:

   Image:                 gcr.io/google_samples/gb-frontend:v3

   Port:     80/TCP

Requests:

cpu:     100m

memory:  100Mi

  Environment:

   GET_HOSTS_FROM:  dns

  Mounts:          <none>

 Volumes:          <none>

Events:

| FirstSeen | LastSeen | Count | From | SubobjectPath | Type | Reason | Message |
|-----------|----------|-------|------|---------------|------|--------|---------|
| --------- | -------- | ----- | ---- | | -------------- | -------- | ------ | ------- |
| 1m | 1m | 1 | {replicaset-controller } | | Normal | SuccessfulCreate | Created pod: frontend-qhloh |
| 1m | 1m | 1 | {replicaset-controller } | | | | |

Normal          SuccessfulCreate    Created  pod:
frontend-dnjpy

 1m          1m         1        {replicaset-controller }
Normal          SuccessfulCreate    Created  pod:
frontend-9si5l

Now, you can check thepods that are brought up:

kubectl get Pods

You must see the Pod information, such as:

| NAME | READY | STATUS | RESTARTS | AGE |
|------|-------|--------|----------|-----|
| frontend-9si5l | 1/1 | Running | 0 | 1m |
| frontend-dnjpy | 1/1 | Running | 0 | 1m |
| frontend-qhloh | 1/1 | Running | 0 | 1m |

You may also verify whether the owner reference of the pod is set to the frontend ReplicaSet. In order to do this, have the yaml of one of the running pods.

kubectl get pods frontend-9si5l -o yaml

Its output will appear similar to this, with the frontend ReplicaSet information set in the metadata OwnerReference field:

apiVersion: v1

kind: Pod

metadata:

creationTimestamp: 2019-01-31T17:20:41Z

generateName: frontend-

labels:

tier: frontend

name: frontend-9si5l

namespace: default

ownerReferences:

  - apiVersion: extensions/v1beta1

blockOwnerDeletion: true

controller: true

kind: ReplicaSet

name: frontend

uid: 892a2330-257c-11e9-aecd-025000000001[15]

# Kubernetes Master Components

Let's have a look at the Kubernetes architecture

---

[15]*ReplicaSet. (2019). Retrieved from* [https://kubernetes.io/docs/concepts/workloads/controllers/replicaset/](https://kubernetes.io/docs/concepts/workloads/controllers/replicaset/)

diagram. Although it may look complex at first, it is not. By the end of the chapter, you will have a clear understanding of the topicand how these components interact with each other.

---

[16]*Jorge Acetozi. Kubernetes Master Components: Etcd, API Server, Controller Manager, and Scheduler. (2017). Retrieved from*

*https://medium.com/jorgeacetozi/kubernetes-master-components-etcd-api-server-controller-manager-and-scheduler-3a0179fc8186*

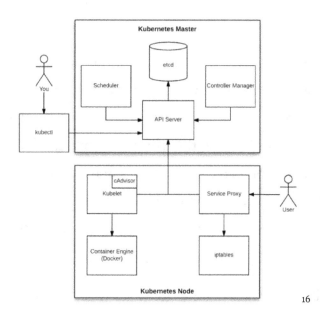

16

The Kubernetes master will run the controller manager, scheduler, API server, and etcd components and it is responsible for managing the Kubernetes cluster. Basically, the master is the brain of the cluster. Now, let's take a look at the components of the master. During production, you need to set up Kubernetes with several clusters for greater availability.

Etcd: This is a consistent key value and distributed

store utilized for configuration management, coordination of distributed work, and service discovery. If it is the question of Kubernetesetcd, it will reliably store the configuration data of the cluster representing its state, such as what nodes are present in the cluster, which pods need to be running, what nodes they are running on, and a lot more at a given point of time.

All the cluster data gets stored in etcd and therefore you must have a back-up plan for the etcd. The etcd data can be easily backed up by using the etcdctl snapshot save command. If you are running your Kubernetes on AWS, it is also possible to take a back-up of the etcd by taking an EBS volume snapshot, as we know etcd is written in Go and makes use of Raft consensus algorithm for managing high-availability replicated logs.

A consensus algorithm called Raft is designed as an alternative to the Paxos. This consensus issue involves several servers agreeing on various values. This is a common issue which arises in the context of replicated state machines. Three various roles are defined by Raft viz. Candidate, Follower, and Leader, and it will achieve consensus through an elected leader. You can find more info about Rafts on the net.

As we know, Etcdctl is a command line interface tool developed by using Go and allows manipulation of the etcd cluster. This may be used for performing a range of actions like setting, updating, and removing keys, verifying cluster health, adding or removing etcd nodes, and generating DB snapshots. You can play around with a five node etcd cluster online.

There is a watch feature available with etcd as well that provides an event-based interface for synchronous monitoring of changes to the keys. When the key is changed, the watchers will be notified. It is a critical feature in the Kubernetes context and the API server components rely heavily on this for getting notified and call the appropriate business logic parts for moving the current state to the desired one.

## *API Server*

When you are interacting with the Kubernetes cluster by using the kubectl command line interface, you will actually be communicating with the API server component. The API server is your most significant management point in the entire cluster. It processes REST operations in short, validates them and updates the corresponding objects in the etcd. The API server serves out the Kubernetes API and is intended to be an easy server relatively. It has almost all business logic implemented in different components or inside plugins. The API server is the only component of Kubernetes that can connect to etcd. All other components need to go through the API server for working with the cluster state.

The API server also happens to be responsible for the authorization and authentication mechanisms. All the API clients need to be authenticated for interacting with the API server. The API servers also implement a watch mechanism similar to the etcd for enabling the clients to watch the changes. It allows components like the scheduler and controller manager the interaction with API servers in a loosely-bound manner.

The pattern is used extensively in Kubernetes. For instance, while you are creating a pod by using kubectl, this is what will happen:

Kubectl will write to the API server. The API server will validate this request and persist it to the etcd. The etcd notifies the API server. The API server will invoke the scheduler. The scheduler will decide where to run the pod and will return this decision back to the API server. The server will persist it to the etcd. The etcd again will notify back to the API server. Now, the API server will invoke the Kubelet in the respective node. The Kubelet will talk to the Docker daemon by using the API over the Docker socket for creating the container. The Kubelet will upload the pod status to your API server and, again, the API server will continue the latest state to etcd.

### *Controller Manager*

The controller manager in Kubernetes is a daemon which embeds the core control loops, also called controllers, which are shipped with Kubernetes. Fundamentally, the controller watches the cluster state via the API server watch feature and, once it is notified, it will make the necessary changes by attempting to move the concurrent state to the required state. Some instances of controllers which are shipped with the Kubernetes are endpoints controller, namespace controller, and replication controller.

Apart from this, the controller manager performs other lifecycle functions like namespace creation and lifecycle, terminated pod garbage collection, event garbage collection, node garbage collection, and cascading deletion garbage collection.

## *Scheduler*

It looks out for the unscheduled pods and binds them with the nodes through the binding pod sub-resource API as per the availability of requested resources, affinity and anti-affinity specs, requirements for the quality of service, and some other constraints. When the pod has the node assigned, the Kubelet's regular behavior will be triggered and the pod with the containers will get created. We have seen the pod creation steps above in the API server section.

# Kubernetes Jobs

The Kubernetes job creates one or more pods and makes sure that a specified number of them are successfully terminated. As the pods are completed successfully, the job will track the successful completion. As a specific number of successful completions are reached, the job is completed. Deleting the jobs will clean up the pod it created.

All this is significant as, by default, Kubernetes tries to get success out of a downhill job. In case it fails, it returns it. If the code is not idempotent, it could mean trouble. Do not fret yet though as there are configuration options available for tuning the behavior. In case your jobs are created as a response to the event-driven queue processing or workflow service, you are looking for the Kubernetes deployment or parallelism rather than a job. The job can be created in one of the two ways viz manually or through the CronJob.

### *Creating a Job Manually*

Under its hood, the pod performs the work for the job. Jobs are abstractions around the pods. Now, to start, open your editor and create a file called job.yaml.

apiVersion: batch/v1

kind: Job

metadata: # metadata for the job

name: pi-job

spec:

template: # template for the pod the job will create

metadata: # metadata for the pod

name: pi-pod

```
spec:

containers:

  - name: pi

image: perl

command:  ["perl",     "-Mbignum=bpi",   "-wle",
"print bpi(2000)"]

restartPolicy: Never

backoffLimit: 4 #This tells kube to run the job 4
times in the event of failure
```

It is an amazing example. Now, create your job.

kubectl create -f ./job.yaml

You may inspect its details with:

kubectl describe jobs/pi

You may inspect the pod as well, which is created
by the job to actually run your workload as:

kc get pods

You will see something like:

READY                          STATUS
RESTARTS   AGE

pi-dfqlv          0/1     Completed      0        1m

Now, let's run it again:

kubectl create -f ./job.yaml

You will, in all probability, get an error message:

Error from server (AlreadyExists): error when creating "./job.yaml": jobs.batch "pi" already exists

It is because just a single instance of a job may exist. In order to get around this, you might either name your job uniquely or you might use CronJob that manages the naming for you. Before going any further, let's delete this job:

kubectl delete jobs/pi

The kubectl will let you know a lot about Kubernetes resources which includes jobs. You can use:

kubectl explain jobs... for getting an overview of YAML configuration.

You may nest the explanation requests with any field Kubernetes can respond with. It is a great way of looking at documentation as you are working on resource definition. The following will show some advanced options for setting on the job:

kubectl explain jobs.spec

You may keep on nesting the calls:

kubectl explain jobs.spec.template

### *CronJob for Creating a Job*

A higher level abstraction in Kubernetes is termed

as CronJob and it creates the jobs in a cron schedule. The CronJob creates jobs, while jobs create pods. You will notice that the job specs for the above are placed below the jobtemplate in this. Open your editor and create a file called cronjob.yaml.

apiVersion: batch/v1beta1

kind: CronJob

metadata:

name: pi-cronjob # this is metadata for the cron service

spec:

schedule: "*/1 * * * *"

jobTemplate:

metadata:

name: pi-job # this is metadata for the job

```
spec:

template:

metadata:

name: pi-pod # this is the metadata for the pod

spec:

containers:

    - name: pi

image: perl

command: ["perl",    "-Mbignum=bpi",   "-wle",
"print bpi(2000)"]

restartPolicy: OnFailure
```

kubectl create -f ./cronjob.yaml

Now, let us list the running cron jobs:

kubectl get cronjob

See this,

| SCHEDULE | SUSPEND | ACTIVE | LAST SCHEDULE | AGE |
|---|---|---|---|---|
| pi*/1 * * * * | False | 1 | 22s | 1m |

Cronjobs will create jobs. Wait for a minute and then go for:

kubectl get jobs

You will see something like:

| | DESIRED | SUCCESSFUL | AGE |
|---|---|---|---|
| pi-1534882380 | 1 | 1 | 2m |
| pi-1534882440 | 1 | 1 | 1m |
| pi-1534882500 | 1 | 0 | 24s |

Pods are created by jobs under the hood for doing the work. Go for:

kubectl get pods

You will see something like this:

| READY | STATUS | RESTARTS | AGE |
|---|---|---|---|
| pi-1534882380-8skhx | 0/1 | Completed | 0 3m |
| pi-1534882440-d7rfj | 0/1 | Completed | 0 2m |
| pi-1534882500-fgjsv | 0/1 | Completed | 0 1m |

Kubernetes, by default, will leave the last three successful pods and one failed pod so that you may inspect their logs and exit status. It is customizable as you can see from the advanced CronJob configuration below. Inevitably, you will be required to run a one-off on the cronjob. Kubernetes also provides support for this.

kubectl create job --from=cronjob/pi-cronjob a-unique-name-for-your-job

Now, for the clean-up:

kubectl delete -f ./cronjob.yaml

And lastly, the fully featured configuration of the cronjob:

apiVersion: batch/v1beta1

kind: CronJob

metadata:

name: pi-cronjob # this is metadata for the cron service

labels:

env: prod

spec: # the CronJob's spec

concurrencyPolicy: Forbid # Allow, Replace, and Forbid are valid options

failedJobsHistoryLimit: 5 # defaults to 1

successfulJobsHistoryLimit: 5 # defaults to 3

startingDeadlineSeconds: 60 # if a job fails to schedule, give it n-seconds of start time leniency

```
schedule: "*/1 * * * *"

jobTemplate:

metadata:

name: pi-job # this is metadata for the job

labels:

env: prod

spec: # the Job's spec

activeDeadlineSeconds: 60 # kill this job if it runs longer than this

backoffLimit: 0 # defaults to 6, attempts kube will make to get an exit 0

template:

metadata:

name: pi-pod # this is metadata for the pod

labels:
```

env: prod

spec: # the pod's spec

containers:

     - name: pi

image: perl

command: ["perl", "-Mbignum=bpi", "-wle", "print bpi(2000)"]

restartPolicy: OnFailure[17]

---

[17]*Working with KubernetesJobs. (2018). Retrieved from* *https://medium.com/coryodaniel/working-with-kubernetes-jobs-848914418*

Akash V.P.

# Chapter 6: Introduction to Some Advanced Kubernetes Topics

## *ConfigMaps*

The ConfigMaps are used to bind command line arguments, configuration files, port numbers, environment variables and other similar configuration artifacts to the pod container and system components at the runtime. The API resource of the config map provides mechanisms for injecting containers with the configuration data, and keeping the container agnostic of Kubernetes. It can also be used to store fine-grained information, such as individual properties or even the coarse-grained information, such as JSON blobs or config files.

### *Resource Quotas*

When many users or a team shares a cluster with a fixed number of nodes, you may feel concerned that one of the users might use up more resources than its fair share. The resource quotas are the administrative tools for addressing this concern. The resource quota is defined by the ResourceQuota object and it provides constraints which limit the overall resource consumption per namespace. The number of objects that can be created in a namespace by type can also be controlled by resource quotas, along with the total number of compute resources consumed by the project.

### *Persistent Volumes*

Managing storage is a different problem than managing the compute. The PersistentVolume subsystem provides the API for the users and the

admin and abstracts the details of how the storage can be provided and how it can be consumed. In order to do this, 2 new API resources will be needed viz. PersistentVolume and PersistentVolumeClaim. The second one allows the users to consume abstract storage resources, but it is more often that the users will need PersistentVolume, having varying properties, like performance, for various issues. The cluster administrators should be capable of offering a range of persistent volumes which differ in several ways, such as access modes and size without actually exposing the users to the details of how the volumes are to be implemented.

### *RBAC*

RBAC long form is Role Based Access Control. It is a method used for regulating the access to a computer or network resources, and it is based on the roles of independent users in an enterprise.

RBAC is an authorization mechanism used for managing permissions around the Kubernetes resources. It permits the configuration of flexible authorization policies which can be updated without the cluster restarts.

### Helm

Helm, basically, is the package manager for Kubernetes. It is the best method for finding, sharing, and using the software built for Kubernetes. It helps you in managing the Kubernetes applications. The helm charts aid you in defining, installing, and upgrading even the most difficult Kubernetes applications. The charts are easy to develop, share, version, and publish so you may stop the copy-paste now and start using Helm. The latest versions are maintained by CNCF in collaboration with Google, Microsoft, Bitnami, and the contributor community.

## *StatefulSet*

It is the workload API object utilized for managing stateful applications. You may define the desired state in a StatefulSet object and the controller of StatefulSet will make the necessary updates for getting there from your current state. It represents a set of pods having unique and persistent identities with stable hostnames which GKE maintains regardless of where they get scheduled. State information and other resilient data for any of the StatefulSet pod get maintained in the persistent disk storage which is associated with the StatefulSet.

## *Load Balancer and Ingress*

Load balancing is a straightforward task in several non-container environments; however, it involves some special handling when containers are involved. The page gathers resources about

configuring and using the Kubernetes load balancer feature. Ingress is an API object which manages the external access to the services in your cluster which is HTTP in the normal course. Apart from SSL termination and name-based virtual hosting, Ingress can also provide load balancing. There is more to the Kubernetes ingress than just the routing rules governing the access to the running services of Kubernetes. In the real world scenario of Kubernetes deployment, there are many additional considerations for managing ingress beyond routing.

# Bibliography

Microservices with Docker and Kubernetes: An Overview. (2018). Retrieved from

*https://opensourceforu.com/2018/05/microservices-with-docker-and-kubernetes-an-overview/*

What does Kubernetes actually do and why use it? (2017). Retrieved from *http://www.developintelligence.com/blog/2017/02/kubernetes-actually-use/*

Install Kubernetes: The Ultimate Guide. (2019) Retrieved from *https://platform9.com/docs/install-kubernetes-the-ultimate-guide/*

*Samarpit*.Understanding Kubernetes Architecture.(2018) Retrieved from *https://www.edureka.co/blog/kubernetes-architecture/*

Understanding Kubernetes Objects (2019).

Retrieved                                              from
_https://kubernetes.io/docs/concepts/overview/w_
_orking-with-objects/kubernetes-objects/_

Jorge Acetozi. Kubernetes Master Components: Etcd, API Server, Controller Manager, and Scheduler. (2017). Retrieved                                              from
_https://medium.com/jorgeacetozi/kubernetes-_
_master-components-etcd-api-server-controller-_
_manager-and-scheduler-3a0179fc8186_

ReplicaSet.        (2019).        Retrieved        from
_https://kubernetes.io/docs/concepts/workloads/_
_controllers/replicaset/_

Working with Kubernetes Jobs. (2018). Retrieved from  _https://medium.com/coryodaniel/working-_
_with-kubernetes-jobs-848914418_

Akash V.P.

Kubernetes Handbook